Are You a Bird?

by THOMAS KINGSLEY TROUPE

illustrated by MARTINA ROTONDO

Hannah was a small, nosy hummingbird. She wanted to learn things. Yesterday, a gnat said an odd word.

"I sure don't like birds," Georgia the gnat whispered.

"What's a bird?" Hannah asked.

"Are you kidding me?" Georgia cried. Then she flew off into the woods.

Hannah wasn't kidding. She DID want to know.

"Where are you going?" Hannah asked.

"Away from these soft little guys," Talulah said. "My job here is done!"

Hannah kept looking. Flying around the lake, she spied Fernando the fish.

"Are you a bird?" Hannah asked.
Fernando's eyes bugged out.
"Oh, my scales!" he said. "I'm not a bird. Birds are warm-blooded!"
"What is your blood like?" Hannah asked.
"Most fish are cold-blooded. Our body temperature matches the water we're in," Fernando said.

He spit water at Hannah.

"Beaks? What for?"

"For eating food."

"But I've got paws and claws for my prrrrey!"

"Whoa!" Hannah yelled, narrowly escaping the cat's claws.

"Birds have wings?" Hannah asked.

"Indeed," Barry said. "But other creatures do too. Only birds have feathers."

She flew over to Bertha the bear, who was sitting in a cave.

ARE YOU A BIRD?

Bertha looked shocked. "A bird? That's really funny," Bertha said. "Most birds have hollow bones."

Hannah would remember hollow bones. Near the swamp, she saw Forrest the frog.

ARE YOU A BIRD?

"Oh, for crying out loud," Forrest said. "I'm not a bird. I have to hop around. I can't fly like you and most birds."

"Not all birds fly?" Hannah asked.

"Nah," Forrest said. "Birds like penguins, ostriches, and emus don't. Little wings, big bodies."

Hannah found herself near a farm. She saw Rusty the rooster strutting around.

"How do you cock-a-doodle-do?" Rusty crowed.
"Wait a second," Hannah called.
"Are you a bird?"
"I am!" Rusty said. "I've got two legs and two wings. That makes me a bird!"

"Hey, you should come to my party!" Rusty invited.

Hannah followed Rusty. She saw animals with feathers. They had beaks. They had two legs and two wings.

"You're all birds!" Hannah cried.

"Yes," Octavia the ostrich said, smiling. "And you are too!"

Hannah looked at herself. She had feathers, a beak, wings, and two legs. She was part of the group, too.

"Of course I am," Hannah chirped.

Hannah's Notes

BIRDS . . .

- Hatch from eggs, which have hard shells.
- Usually stay with their eggs to keep them warm until they are hatched.
- Are warm-blooded.
- Have beaks.
- Have feathers.
- Have two wings.
- Usually have hollow bones.
- Have two legs.

GLOSSARY

beak The pointed mouth of a bird; beaks are hard with different shapes depending on what birds eat.

cold-blooded Having a body temperature that changes to match the surrounding temperature.

feathers One of the light, soft parts that cover a bird's body.

hollow Empty inside, like a straw.

warm-blooded Having a body temperature that stays about the same no matter what the air temperature is.

wing One of the parts of an animal's body that it uses to fly.

WEBSITES

American Bird Conservancy: The Diverse World of Bird Beaks

https://abcbirds.org/blog/bird-breaks/

BioKids—Kids' Inquiry of Diverse Species—Birds

http://www.biokids.umich.edu/critters/Aves/

Birds: National Geographic Kids

https://kids.nationalgeographic.com/animals/birds

Every effort has been made to ensure that these websites are appropriate for children. However, because of the nature of the Internet, it is impossible to guarantee that these sites will remain active indefinitely or that their contents will not be altered.

READ MORE

Anthony, William. *Birds.* Minneapolis: Jump, 2024.

Jaycox, Jaclyn. *Unusual Life Cycles of Birds.* Mankato, Minn.: Capstone, 2022.

Rathburn, Betsy. *Brilliant Birds.* Minneapolis: Bellwether, 2023.

AMICUS ILLUSTRATED is published by
Amicus Learning, an imprint of Amicus
P.O. Box 227, Mankato, MN 56002
www.amicuspublishing.us

Copyright © 2025 Amicus. International copyright reserved in all countries. No part of this book may be reproduced in any form without written permission from the publisher.

Library of Congress Cataloging-in-Publication Data
Names: Troupe, Thomas Kingsley, author. | Rotondo, Martina, illustrator.
Title: Are you a bird? / by Thomas Kingsley Troupe ; illustrated by Martina Rotondo.
Description: Mankato, MN : Amicus Illustrated, [2025] | Series: Animal classification | Includes bibliographical references. | Audience: Ages 6–9 | Audience: Grades 2–3 | Summary: "When nosy Hannah the hummingbird overhears Georgia the gnat saying she doesn't like birds, Hannah sets out on a mission to find out what exactly a bird is. After interviewing other animals and learning about the characteristics of birds, Hannah realizes that she too is a bird! Includes fact page, glossary, and resources for further research"—Provided by publisher.
Identifiers: LCCN 2024010600 (print) | LCCN 2024010601 (ebook) | ISBN 9798892001144 (library binding) | ISBN 9798892001724 (paperback) | ISBN 9798892002301 (ebook)
Subjects: LCSH: Birds—Juvenile literature. | Birds—Classification—Juvenile literature. | Animals—Classification—Juvenile literature.
Classification: LCC QL676.2 .T66 2025 (print) | LCC QL676.2 (ebook) | DDC 598.01/2—dc23/eng/20240404
LC record available at https://lccn.loc.gov/2024010600
LC ebook record available at https://lccn.loc.gov/2024010601

Printed in China

Editor: Rebecca Glaser
Designer: Kim Pfeffer

ABOUT THE AUTHOR
Thomas Kingsley Troupe is the author of more than 200 books for young readers. When he's not writing, he enjoys reading, playing video games, and investigating haunted places with the Twin Cities Paranormal Society. Otherwise, he's probably taking a nap or something. Thomas lives in Woodbury, Minnesota, with his two sons.

ABOUT THE ILLUSTRATOR
Artist since always, Martina Rotondo attended the Master of Illustration and Concept Art at The Sign Academy in Florence, Italy. She currently works as an illustrator for both Italian and foreign publishing houses. Lover of traditional drawing, she is also constantly researching and experimenting with new techniques to create her surreal and engaging characters and backgrounds.